a lesson in smallness

a lesson in smallness

lauren goodwin slaughter

The National Poetry Review Press
Aptos, California

The National Poetry Review Press
(an imprint of DHP)
Post Office Box 2080, Aptos, California 95001-2080

a lesson in smallness

Printed in the United States of America
Published in 2015 by The National Poetry Review Press

ISBN 978-1-935716-37-2

CONTENTS

~For Ben, Sam, and Eleanor

~And, for Eleanor Johnson Lindner
(as promised)

I.

MIGRATION

1.

Tell me again of the flounder's eye—
I liked your demonstration

using an olive and a tennis ball
to show how one eye roams

over the top of the head
till adjacent to its twin—from normal

swimming to lateral flat,
so for the rest of their lives left side

equals up. Love, have we flipped
from bottom feeder too fast?

You wear a suit to work, trading in
the worn Carhartts for Jos. A. Bank;

I put on a cardigan and teach.
On occasion, yes, even lipstick.

Tell me again that we'll live in a cabin.
Make me a necklace of sea glass.

2.

Or, don't.
We are here with our hardwood floors,

our muscular mixing-appliances,
a patio with shade-loving plants,

ecological light-bulbs. In Italy,
when I was growing our own

evolving son, I could not eat
the unpasteurized Mozzarella di Buffala.

You compared me to Francesca
swirling in romantic infinitude,

forbidden to eat the soft exquisite

cheese. Yes, I still like it
when you touch me.

Touch me. Then,
to paint the nursery.

THE BAREFOOT CONTESSA

makes Panna Cotta using one whole vanilla-bean.
Fridays, Jeffrey finds his way home to East Hampton,

trailing the sigh of Perfect Roast Chicken—
the plumpest birds come from Iaconos' farm.

The day is perfectly blustery as he speeds
down the driveway—leaf piles whoosh and suspend.

Every low-watt bulb in the house glows
inwardly—a gentle thrill just for him.

Jeffrey's jacket is off, tie loose.
The red door slo-mo opens itself

to a hall of cocked family-photos—
each grin goes: *someone loves me.*

Not a bad idea: find work in the city,
come home to your needs filled just as they growl

for Lamb Provencal and Mocha Chocolate Icebox Cake.
Jeffrey reaches for his glass just as Ina

appears with the open burgundy to fill it.
She cooks only with what she would drink.

THE BAREFOOT CONTESSA WAKES UP WITH
THAT TOO-FULL FEELING

Probably nothing.
Exactly what was said?

She has a sense they looked
into her and saw. Hors d'oeuvres

of melon wrapped in the thinnest
prosciutto. Prosecco. Air

is a clog of meat drippings.
Downstairs, violet hydrangeas

from an orb of glass bow
onto the splattered tablecloth.

Their heads might just fall off.

Best to stay in bed. Best to wait.
How the chicken grease pollution

will cling to her robe, re-infect
her hair when she gathers

the necessary oomph. Not yet.
Lovely, though, to think

of the place settings: a sugar cookie
frosted with each guest's name: *Angela*.

Days burn into gummy
sleep—exploding

kindred, splintered
spoon-lakes, vicious gulls

and mean, sweaty carnivals.
I'm jealous of your dreams;

kites lift you over oceans,
each phosphorescent fish

a mirrored hinge
of constellation. Some nights

you're hired just to sit at diners
and eat endless plates of eggs.

So here—

press your forehead
to mine like a goat.

HERCULANEUM

1.

The wells are done and the oranges over.
Overlapping stone, dust. Silence

whips between the walls and streets.
I see an urn that hands grasped.

So. We are here. And the Swedish
family in crisp bandanas, a flushed

Floridian, a red sea of kid shirts,
as a woman leans against a column

nursing her sweaty child.
Her watch spotlights the improbable

Roman shopkeeper's sign.
Like the teens' cell phones pitched

too high: the past wails a place
beyond bounds. Above the excavation,

a new town—

laundry from balconies
like children crossing the street.

2.

In a too-British voice the audio tour
points us toward The House of the Genius

with its broken Cupid candlestick,
to the Villa of the Papyri's

carbonized scrolls and frescos
of immortal Hercules,

who was once too strong to master the lyre
and with one dumb blow killed the tutor

he loved. In House #22, a mosaic:
teal ocean curls behind

Amphitrite and Neptune—gold
sex spills off each small square.

3.

The boathouse is the resting place
of the Ring Lady, named for the circles

still round her bones. She tried to breathe
in the gas first, the voice says, ash, then so much

rock flying. From her pelvis the experts
understood how many children she bore.

Whose faces looked to her before the air jammed?
What softness could her hands not find?

SEAHORSE

The coronet is distinctive
as a thumbprint—pressed in ink

it reminds me of an atom waterfall.
I want to know the smallness

of your life—

pectoral, dorsal fins that quaver
you through plankton waves

and zodiacs of jellyfish.
These must be your eggs

of revelation. Do you
and your mate glisten

petite questions to the ocean?
The distilled moon?

Tides pull you in cyclones, tails
curled around sea sticks

holding on for heart's cause—
one eye to the urchin, blooming,

the other to your weightless
darling—in soundless bells

you sleep like that, in kites.
It's gorgeous how you make

your little clan, the zygotes slipped
inside the pouch, his, as if

they were a passed note
or a kiss. Say that's us.

BELLY

I'm tired, she says. We're sleeping, he says.

Who knew a beginning could be totally quiet.

Leaf-light, footprints, a strand of hair blowing past.

Uneven bells, the traveling.

Mushrooms pushing from the earth.

II

THE BAREFOOT CONTESSA IS GLAD
SHE NEVER HAD CHILDREN

On a night like tonight: the patio, tea candles,
guests rosy and sleepy. Such a feast

eating almost seemed a burden. Almost.

Casual—*wear a polo*—just burgers
by the pool. (Ground sirloin topped

with the best blue cheese, arugula, and still-warm
heirlooms from her garden. Then wow

them—why not—with eight personal
chocolate pecan-pies.) To make others

feel exceptional—this her gift—these
tipsy neighbors with pastel sweaters

around their necks. And her husband,
pausing now over one final glass.

Ella and a light plank through
the open kitchen window disperse.

Any longer on this chair she'll be lattice.

REQUIRED READING

As per the book,
balloons pop a child

opens and sucks
lodging in his windpipe

a piece you can't remove.
(Carrots, hotdogs, a loose button.)

Disregard grapes,
he dies.

HIS EYES ON THE SPARROW

1.

Our neighbor Kenny, two, fell
into the pool

just like that.

2.

At the service

I was good and did not fuss
about the wool

too-tight tights
or patent-leather shoes

that made me want
to eat.

3.

White carnations

like cake flowers
all over the church.

4.

I worried
about his teeth.

Mine, I kept
in a ballerina music box

with a ring and pictures
of my cat.

5.

I wondered

what clothes
his mother put him in—

hoped for a yellow sleeper
feet unzipped

so he wouldn't get too hot.

6.

As the hymn began—

I sing because I'm happy
I sing because I'm free—

with a little noise
my own mom seized me.

BY WHAT AGE SHOULD THE BABY SPEAK FLUENT CHINESE

The itsy bitsy spider's
a goner. This land is now

just yours. Get up, ashes

ashes or not and row
this boat like you mean it.

PAINTING THE NURSERY

Will we fall like a comet?

Orbit forever in a horsetail

of sleep, dust and fire?

KING CAKE BABIES

In the junk drawer of receipts,

sour corks, and used prescriptions

a Ziploc keeps her stash

of airless prizes: the brown one

with no eyes, the yellow baby

beaming like a salesman.

Babies, rows and rows of them

cook inside clear beeping boxes.

The sandy-eyed parents in the NICU

know better but linger before triplets

born at twenty-two weeks—trinkets

in afghans grandmothers stitched.

The hummingbird's nest

is made of lichens, spider-webs,

and soft leaves stowed above a stream

to guard against hawks. Each moment

is a lesson in smallness.

THE RIVER

When I say yes, it's one
-hundred in the house

if nothing moves. Been breathing

ink, mosquitoes, bad adjectives,
so a canoe trip sounds good.

A blue afternoon
down shoals massages calm—

will float even, cool—the perfect story.

So as muddy, brown hands
become waves on the river, the river

six feet higher than usual, I click
on my jacket, think *retching, hag-like,*

vertiginous, jump
into the boat and push off

leaving everyone on shore (they love me,
they want to smell my hair). Addlepates, I go

as a log thugs the bow and the whole boat
stutters. I just bobble on

somewhere, one paddle,

knuckles bleached.

Ahead, a bird sees a fish.
Dives in. Gets it. Flies off. Eats.

ICE BONE

~For Edward, in memory

Say the black road
is a bleached crest raveling

the one distance
meant for you (all of us).

Turn the stars
that night into light

animals. Aspirin moon
in its place glowing

over an ice bone
sea, the lives of your yellow

blanket thrown over
(hush). Make it August

(our summer) in Maine. Warm
stolen beer, adult beer

—Heineken—your mouth
on the bottle, my shoulder

my nipple (making out
to a manual—your boy-smell

is Camels, Ivory soap). We sailed
over clearness

in your small, white boat.
Take the tank top

I wore—its cool
Indian design—the pattern

paste it to this map
of—(your hand)—nodded off

at the wheel—I hear
the obit names you "seaman"

you'd become a (cigar box
—sea shells and snap

shots—the whale postcard
signed LOVE YOU) captain

summed up, wrapped around everything   .
now (a cement truck).

M.A.N.N.A.

---

*Metropolitan Area Neighborhood Nutrition Alliance, Saint
Vincent's Church*

The signal on my inheritance,
a rusty green Taurus, clicked

cornering on to Duval,
my right arm karate-chopped

against the pothole-shifted
stack of greenhouse boxes.

Squares of meaty lasagnas,
like neckless power-lifters,

and mounds of veggie confetti
jiggled free of the sisters' clean

divisions. Each trash lump
in the road was a dead family

dog. The wind a screeching
Septa bus, I got out at Ms. Gordon's;

an apparition behind a peach
curtain, she tapped

to put hers on the welcome mat—
a cat-piss carpet scrap.

Two doors down, widower Fountain
had the darkness punched

into his sockets. His daughter hoped
for shortcake, her favorite.

Mrs. Arbus, in the buckled shack,
was last because she could hold me

on her cobwebby stoop forever (too-far
from the car still smoky

with my mother), retelling the horror
of needles and paychecks, her son

locked up and her husband who left
for some *bitch*. Sister Barbara

has a bowling-bag purse
spilling peppermints and little green Bibles,

I recalled, as fingernail talons
met at my back and dug, cleaving

me into Mrs. Arbus—her forsaken breasts
and jutting thorax. But-thank-God-for-you

twist around my neck and I wanted to say
Manna is just something I'm trying,

not even a commitment, like last month's
shelter and next week's cure race, but Mrs. Arbus

is a drowner who can only hear the tuba
plug of her own voice as it sinks

down too fast to the undiscovered ships
crawling with lightlessness and claws

at whatever happens to be standing,

which today is me kicking those rusty hooks off
my violet sundress, the rippling surface.

GALILEO

Walking to Galileo's home outside of Florence

1.

In coral light we start
the ascent, ancient walls glazing

our backs, the uncertain
landscape echoing

variant green shades.
Dew and lemons

glass air. (How new
I once was, sure

of what I cried for.) Breathing

wisteria up this first rise,
our cobblestone street

comets.

2.

The reason for this is stars,
but what good are stars in daylight?

Women dress as dark dolls,
sweep into the church with their baskets.

I had a dream once (this: I was my own
child at my breast and kept switching

her mouth—nipple to nipple—
woke swollen, aching,

the same) of wax. We are here
on the street. Sun is a place.

IN SALERNO

I like the honey but not the fish.
Toast is mean with anchovies—

a million tiny eyeballs glaring,
Who are you? What are you doing here?

I knife their small exaggerated
faces, pop their eyes like grapes.

It doesn't work. *Tis-tis* they click
in a rain-roof voice, *tis-tis.*

BIOPSY (CHESTNUT HILL HOSPITAL)

Under the spotlight

in an empty theater
my father and I

wait for Mom's nurse.
The wall clock sucks

its ticks back
into the silence wondering

at that smeary sailboat
print—there seems to be no water.

The endless splayed copies of Prevention stutter

Walk off the Weight, Walk off the Weight. . .

So much is gone, even
her eyebrows.

Dad must keep
ten kinds of bird seed.

On the muted T.V.
smoke clarifies that that

office building just collapsed
with untold stories inside.

As if there was no backyard hawk,
every morning he hauls out those bags.

APPOINTMENT AT THE FERTILITY CLINIC

The horses in Texas are starving.
Still on the couch, I watch one keeper

tell of eyeglasses and the cable T.V.
she forgoes just to try to pay for the hay.

The story zooms into a sweaty kid
skidding sadly down a slide.

From her freak cherry mouth,
the blonde helmet reports each night

a new thin horse gets abandoned
in this local park: close-up of dust,

the gray thin horse licking dirt.
Thin horses suck flies into their eyes.

The skin of thin horses pushed up
oversized sleeves. What child wants

a new thin horse? Gasping bones
thin horses want infinite greening

pastures wrapped around them and around
them, around, around, around.

ROMANTIC MOVIES

1.

The plane crashed, but did the pilot
have to be so badly burned?

Our blonde—her hair fluent, sea plants reaching
for the sea—must she love him so

no matter what? Wailing in silence
by carlight at the hospital, he's strapped

down by puzzling contraptions.

2.

Should I slip on my slip

and rush for this flight or wait
full-blushed for the boarding call?

LAURA, AFTER HER MOTHER'S STROKE

There is a cloth
I can soak with clear water

to put on your broken forehead,
Laura. Laura, my oldest friend.

She's still here

I offer but your yowl is a fin
that cuts through everything

in this room. She's not. A black mountain

photograph tilts above the couch—
one of those stock prints knocked off

by the thousands. The spanning next moment is a field
of me trying—

You're exhausted, you need to sleep.
I hear myself say: Sleep now.

Watch my arms put the shawl on Laura's shoulders.

Thousands and thousands of these black mountains.

WELCOME TO PARADISE

~For Shug

1.

It's glut & the throat
bloat again on this cut-

glass morning—sailclouds
jab the wavetops

as we sludge sand,
brimming still

from last night's
indulgence: skewered

jumbo shrimp-&-chorizo,
fried oysters, calamari.

Because I said I'd try but didn't, ·
the lone tentacle O-ed

from my plate.

2.

As Ben and I sunned, his grandmother
—barely post-stroke—ate

by the tube in her gut,

bright flowers on the shelf

on her "good side." "Gorgeous!"

the nurse in her native gold
tone spoke Caribbean hoops.

All hospitals are named for a saint.

3.

The brochure read, *Welcome to Paradise!*

Over dinner, we tried to make the decision as the sea
voiced-over
our voices—

oily Tiki-torches illuminating
us.

They found her
on the floor. Who knew

how long she'd been there, her fist
a curling claw?

4.

The soft-shelled crab's shell is too soft.

Evolution or greasy preparation?

Go ahead, soothe your belly
with some other armor—

devour an animal's mustard,
lick the plate clean.

5.

The saint's halo

is a mechanical scoop
that just digs the damn thing out.

As a rule, intact eyeballs
on roasted whole fish

are the part saveurs spoon first.

6.

Shrivel distant palm trees.

The ten-ish beach boy wants to show us

his jellyfish
clumped in a yellow-castle pail.

"Each one has three separate bodies,"

he brags, as the visored parent-heads
beam behind him.

"Beautiful," I go.

"But dangerous," he corrects.

7.

Afforded me…

—Shug starts, unstuck now

as the eye & the ocean

narrows & swells—

…You have afforded me great pleasure.

The room fills
with room for nothing else.

III.

IMAGE MAKERS SALON AND DAY SPA

Tuscaloosa, Alabama

It's enough to make one's eyes peel—
this veil of florid chemicals

peroxide, gel, and aerosol
knit with perfumes called Happy,

Bazar, Obsession, Bali Dream.
Old copies of People

and Southern Living make pillars
on every free surface. (Brangelina

picks an orphan up
again. Paula Deen fries

things.)

I sit down and apologize.
It's been too long, my blonde

is gone,
I keep swimming for miles

and miles and miles
letting it dry by sticking my head

out the window as I whip past
the businesses, schools, and children,

flipping for the right tune
with my right hand,

shooing off clouds with the left.
To confess

the ends are broken
would just be ridiculous.

FRIEND REQUEST

Palm fronds slice
(Montego?) the gulf

blue behind you
and your lovely captives.

Twins! Congratulations,
each smile is a game show

called Denial. She's beautiful
as a wife in an apricot bikini

floating endlessly toward
you. Love Christmas

at your mom's, all those gifts
ripped open. Great you splurged

on a bouncy-house birthday—
those kids were really ricocheting!

Our hangovers boomed
as we burned on the jetty,

getting whipped by wave-tips
that morning. The Wawa

powdered doughnuts
and my favorite violet sundress

were too sugary
for you. Under the Bridge

blared as I failed
to peel out in my junky Geo.

But did you click
to see my own two blue-eyed boys?

TONIGHT

thin leaves of volt and streetlight
sheen into the city pot—

a bouillon, balsamic

with the stuff of subways. I buoy
down the stairs—a mouth

of dusty steel and bodies,

metallic salt of stranger eyes,
limp brushings, mites of conversations:

"I ate," "the NASDAQ," "loves me."

A performer loads the train—
his song fills the car

with wedding veils,
the juicy recollections, onions,

of lives as commuters find truth
on Kindles.

These fast black mirror windows.

Capsule hums, each soul another stop
on my walk home alone. Night knows.

Dewy chandeliers of city.
All solitudes are starry.

WHEN I ARRIVE HOME
FROM THE AIRPORT

Arranged blooms on the mantel.
Your morning piss froths in the toilet: a sign

to ignore your gifts? These lilacs, this
Miro book—his blotches organ-shaped

as if to suggest (since we don't
see them) ours exist? We embrace a bit.

My lips a bell on your neck, I note
the kitchen is not a mess (does this cancel

out the piss?) In fact, each mug is hung
by hook like a dress on the rack—

blue, yellow, pink. Our bed—
when you take my same-sized hand

and steer me there—is made so fluffily.
My book has not been chewed

by the dog we don't have. But the light bulbs
are wrong—too dim—or—you've lit candles:

everywhere:on the shelf, your folding chair—
striking bright tapestries dangling

for curtains, worried in waves with each
small breeze—stars burst—and the room

pulses wax—black holes, galaxies—oh—
you're right here. Note the firefly

of your eyebrow, note the flame lick
of my hair. Now I sense fire—

does that mean I can kiss the parts of you
I want and the gawkers will chalk it up to fear?

To something spiraling? Burning? Now
you're using your hands to makes shadows

a swan. It's crooning at us. I smell work and smoke
in your beard. Now you feel warm to me.

They took their free popcorn
and marched off into

the field suddenly,
as if there'd been a signal.

I saw them all find someone
waiting to stand next to.

The land was wide, weed-flowered.
Assemblies of pinwheels

sky-knived and a boy
blew fists of phantom

dandelions, spilled red
Kool Aid on his shirt.

I watched parents
lay out blankets

in self-contained
squares, weighing the edges

with shoes, knapsacks. One family
linked hands, tumbled

down (sparklers fizzed)
as the camouflaged man rose

from his lawn chair pointing
too soon and two punk rock

teens made out—*Superstar*—
her cheesy top swore,

silver glitter loops
like the pilots' routes

shrunk to the arc
of something small; one body

instead of atmosphere,
one single breathing plain.

White goats scramble up the hill
while on the bus we blunder

cameras out the window, point
to the tracks of what may have been

something. Sticky kids eat, play
miniature games, their beeps

synchro-tuned to our slow reverse
into the designated moose

sojourn. Everyone sunscreens,
plods out, shields, sighs and huffs

back in. Since nothing. Except
the woman in her pink cartoon

Florida visor taps my shoulder,
asks could I please run

down quick, go down
to take a picture of that moose—

her husband's never seen one
—his heart and he's too hot—

and oh how her knees are killing
(will I be a hero)? There's zero

but take this—I'm suddenly a blanket
of white fur movie flowing

and bolt off the lot into
the stretching field before us—

Find the embankment, clamber it.
Go down to the river

to wait. Eat berries
I know, investigate plant leaves,

my hooves, ticks, and lick.
Centuries kaleidoscope

and I forget pillows.

I'm simply in this forest to eat
wait, eat, wait,

sleeping inside light cups
until the moose no longer exists.

EXPERT ADVICE

Well, there's the rain whamming
wail in your chest—it's all scraped

gravel in there, scared to bare, finger
-nailed peach. Vessels squish,

liver's gushing diesel, stomach hole
is lined with sore tentacles (what a bright

shade of purple!). I've seen this before. First
the heart concedes (pumps glooming, ink)

then the rest. Lungs freeze to rocks, organs
squirm inside out, skin fizzes, eyes, lips, nipples

deflate. If you think of the moon
does that help? Not even a blue moon?

Now cough.

Oh, that's bad—those screws are supposed
to remain intact. Deep breath—odd, Rilke's

Apollo lodged in like that. One lozenge
will zap all faith in it and this warm salve

mimics the sunset. Stop! Your reflexes
(thank God) aren't shot—never had

a knee hit a rose like that. You seem ready
to flee at the very least.

But where will you go? Where will you go?

His knapsack of gold light
unzips, flooding the room

with earnestness.

The old moon-clock ticks.

On the couch, this boy of maybe
seventeen shifts

zits and pamphlets.

A ring from his ice water
slips from the glass table.

I wear a dress of black leather.

My hair is spiked and has a pink stripe.
My hip boots zip and zip.

Not really, not really.

Leaning towards him,

I've tried.

SPRING

The worst were the young
dragged in at night,

blind and wailing, destined
to die no matter what we did.

Still, I'd grab the killer cat
as you'd scoop up the finch

and place it on the porch
by the Peace Lily.

Once recovered from shock,
we kept telling ourselves,

it will fly away.

SUNSET ON CLARK FORK

Day's end smudged by coral clouds with the gray-
green movement

of Clark Fork. I walk beside the river
on a gravel path lifting

                  with each step—

A small rock knocks an iridescent beetle
onto its closed wings. I could right it,

but leave it to itself.

A heron stares from the opposite shore—her airy
glim, a column.

Half-way across, antlers like driftwood
hooked with a brown glass bottle

and a clump of some animal's muddy straw home
tease water

figures.   Dusk

feels my arm as the clouds
into cloud more briskly

to shapes ticking.

By the time I reach the leggy old footbridge,

a certain stillness
has settled on each swerve

of beam and drill and a tree
burnt by initials.

The hue from before is a ribbon, faintly waving
forth off the gloaming

line   —a show on the rust cut-across

on the rope metal
where a spider chases
a smaller spider through the veil of below

river, this river, the river—

The heron I know is a sear
in the secret of where I was—she takes off

to make place   in the future
a space

around not now
but sooner now to itself

the closed purple
                              crocus leaves

its own moment
on the other side of the bank.

THREE RIVERS

1.

The world piped green
introspective—paused as if following

some oiled brawl. Each street lamp is its own
thinking underpainting cashmere

cloud on cloud.   A boy walks
noiseless down the middle,

alarming. The bus stop sleepwalks,
dreams of one waiting,   needles

burn into grass. Spanning   breaks
the rise—
buzzed carves   out
flushed strobe—

to gravel lines leading towards
azure.   Such beautiful shining

just to leave it so to seem again
(slicks harden—you're (re)gaining—).

2.

On dawn window arrow
wing-beat suspended

more than unsound is the end
to this season's pelletal shallow—

                         shadowed river,
floating skeletal
                    wisp, stone-thrown
exposed circles

curl warm the celestial
sheet undone—(lip)—moving then actually

doing it.   One day
nothing skips.
One day bird stays put someone

takes a damn, clears it.   Away
now.   Lines are water   All animal. Or
another

recollection then—
silver bound.

3.

Then sunup's projectile

lemon. Then windowsill

space out moving the sweet
spin lit—(split lip)—ripped

core like this star
actually lives here.   Out
there

cities fail as blocks go shady,
          leave

more shapes and bellies   open
somewhere.   Tell me

gently. Tell the secret just so
(just so-so)
the moment's not missing.
          Say so

it stays on the gleam and dream the spot
to its feet—into the cerulean
(O light blanket).

PAPER RAIN; ALABAMA TORNADO OF APRIL 27, 2011

To conclude—I announce what comes after me.
—*Walt Whitman*

A speeding
ticket, a check

stub, a mortgage
slip, *tampons,*

Q-tips, onions, sandwich
stuff on the rip

of a store-list
rained.

Ten million
cubic yards

of battered
brides—

their first time
out of Culman

County—flipped
in the wind

with someone's
hazy femur

x-ray, a report card,
an ultrasound,

an Over the Hill
birthday card.

A crumpled farmer
reclining

with his blue
-ribboned colt—

Good girl, good girl—

blew through the woven
strawlight.

FOSSIL

~For Ben

Finished as the granite,
we're down to our indents

now: pull your hand
from the rock & I'll dust

off the fernish armature
resembling our backs. Hello.

Remember?

How far did the grooves
groove the roads on top

of roads as in Fierenze
with the curb a mile from the mortar?

Why so much stone here?
How far did we ride our habits

& with what weight of stubbornness?
At least our children shone & grew

to be tall doctors (not rock stars),
got a vista from our counsel, vitamins

from my/our cooking. Where are you?
My hair got short—a poof—to remind

us of the past, of missing things—
that something's left at all. Wait,

that's schmaltz. Return the mane—
a braid could last us a morning.

AUGUST

Forces sky down
like a French press

over the boil. Constant cloud
covers thunder—lightning

but no rain—a tease without
the reprieve of a drop—

lonely as the kiss you want
to need but don't. Inside

is no better: a sluggish throb
and sour: sprout bread, green oranges,

cockroaches.

Our newly wound moon-clock
gives up. Lamps hum off.

Books open themselves
like any woman in a skirt

who spreads her legs to the fan
when no one's looking.

We exhale, try and try
to touch each other.

Running space between
our bodies is that water.

MERMAID

1.

She does not believe even in herself—
the first prismatic glimpse

of scale caught in the bathroom
mirror, flake of rainbow

she mistakes for a weird scab.
Given to picking, she takes the Bic

to it, but it bleeds blue and doubles.
Another, another—

Her skin is peach from the shower's
heat, her hair smells of Pantene.

2.

From there to here's a blur. Sky
-scraper horizons then anemone

fields, jellyfish swirling as snow
once did—carillon orchestras

without noise. It is this absence
of sound she loves and misses

most—jackhammer at dawn,
another screaming child.

Somehow she made it to the sea.
Something carried her—full-finned.

I can't even hear myself think
she'd complained, the mystery

now toned as a steal beam
drum: Will I survive? This current

I'm riding, does it feel? Tunnel
of water through water.

Mist and foam, white travel.
There is some place we belong.

ACKNOWLEDGMENTS

42opus: "August," "Ice Bone," "Fossil" ("Fossiling"), "Romantic Movies"

Big Bell: "Expert Advice" ("Hypochondriac")

Birmingham Magazine: "Paper Rain; Alabama Tornado of April 27, 2011"

Blackbird: "Welcome to Paradise"

Blue Mesa Review: "Three Rivers"

Chariton Review: "Appointment at the Fertility Clinic," "By What Age Should the Baby Speak Fluent Chinese," "Required Reading" ("Air"), "The Barefoot Contessa," "The Barefoot Contessa Wakes Up with that Too-Full Feeling," "The Barefoot Contessa is Glad She Never Had Children," "Biopsy (Chestnut Hill Hospital)," "Laura, After Her Mother's Stroke" ("Sarah, After Her Mother's Stroke")

Cimarron Review: "Painting the Nursery" ("Chambers of the Heart") and "The River" ("Blackwater River, Alabama")

Crab Orchard Review: "Air Show" and "National Park"

Controlled Burn: "Galileo"

Dossier: "Image Makers Salon and Day Spa"

Ducts: "Spring"

Fugue: "Osmosis"

Hayden's Ferry: "When I Arrive Home from the Airport"

Hunger Mountain: "Belly," "Herculaneum," "His Eyes on the Sparrow"

The Journal: "Seahorse" and "Tonight"

Juked: "The Book of Mormon"

Kenyon Review Online: "Migration"

Red Mountain Review: "Sunset on Clark Fork"

Salt Hill: "Mermaid"

Verse Daily: "Osmosis"

"The Barefoot Contessa" includes recipe titles and references from Ina Garten's *The Barefoot Contessa Cookbook*, published by Clarkson Potter/Publishers, 1999.

"Expert Advice" references "The Archaic Torso of Apollo" by Rainer Maria Rilke.

Thank you to Jason Morris for donating, "Asprin moon" to the poem, "Ice Bone."

I would like to extend my thanks to the many people who

offered the guidance and criticism that helped so much in the writing of these poems: Robin Behn, Joel Brower, Claudia Emerson, William Logan, Ander Monson, Daniel Torday, Bruce Smith, Dave Smith, and Adam Vines. Thank you, Erin Belieu, for your early encouragement and support. Particular thanks to C.J. Sage for selecting this manuscript.

Thank you to the Rona Jaffe Foundation for their generous support, and also to the Vermont Studio Center and the Sewanee Writers' Conference.

Deepest gratitude to my family for believing in my work, always.

And thanks to Ben. (*Say that's us.*)